PHONICS

ACTIVITIES

Sandra Fisher
Carole Palmer
Susan Bloom
Joyce Stirniman

CONSULTANT
Elizabeth C. Stull, Ph.D.

ILLUSTRATOR
Anne Kennedy

PUBLICATIONS INTERNATIONAL, LTD.

Elizabeth C. Stull holds a doctorate in early and middle childhood education specializing in curriculum and supervision. She has taught language, literacy, and children's literature at Ohio State University and has written numerous activity books for teachers, including *Alligators to Zebras: Whole Language Activities for the Primary Grades, Kindergarten Teachers Survival Guide,* and *Multicultural Learning Activities: K–6.*

Sandra Fisher (M.A.) works at Kutztown University (PA) as an assistant professor of elementary education and coordinator of the Early Learning Center. She has more than 25 years of classroom experience and has served as vice president of the National Organization of Campus Development Laboratory Schools and as editor of the *NOCDLS Bulletin.*

Carole Palmer (M.A.) is a reading specialist. Previously a first-grade teacher, she writes educational material for children, including curricula for reading programs, spelling series, and phonics projects.

Susan Bloom (M.A.) is a writer and editor for Creative Services Associates, Inc., a publisher of educational materials.

Joyce Stirniman is a writer and editor for Creative Services Associates, Inc. She has also served as field manager for the National Assessment of Education Progress—The Nation's Report Card.

Louis Weber, CEO
Publications International, Ltd.
7373 North Cicero Avenue
Lincolnwood, Illinois 60712

Manufactured in U.S.A.

8 7 6 5 4 3 2 1

ISBN: 1-4127-1072-3

CONTENTS

FIRST WORDS

Children soak up knowledge like sponges. This can make it difficult for parents and other educators to know how best to begin teaching children to read. One of the most effective methods for teaching reading is the phonics way.

With the phonics method, the child learns that sounds correspond to alphabet letter symbols. Using these letter sounds, words can be "decoded" and read. The phonics activities in this book are

designed so the child will be learning by "doing," by using senses, and by asking questions. The book is intended for preschoolers, ages three to six, but children slightly younger and older can benefit from the book's activities as well.

To stimulate the child's interest in reading, you must provide a print-rich environment filled with books, magazines, and newspapers. It is important that the child sees you reading

and that you read to the child for pleasure. For practical purposes and for use with this book, it is a good idea to make letter cards: Print the uppercase and lowercase forms of one letter on each of 26 index cards.

Oral communication is also important for language development. Listen to what the child is saying. Talk with him or her as much as possible. With you as a role model, the child will develop good listening and speaking patterns and an interest in learning and reading.

This book is divided into seven chapters. Each chapter has activities designated as "easy" (one star), "medium" (two stars), or "challenging" (three stars). These activity levels

easy	*medium*	*challenging*

are built on the hierarchy of language and reading development.

The "easy" level lays the foundation for basic skills; children manipulate objects and call attention to beginning sounds of words.

On the "medium" level, the child begins to associate letter symbols and letter sounds through listening skills, letter recognition, and tactile experiences. The activities on the "challenging" level require applying letter symbols to letter sounds and using fine motor skills. Children learn at different rates. You may find that the child needs an easier or more challenging activity from one chapter to another.

As you preview these activities, remember that they need not be done in a sequential manner. You should alternate activities, skipping from chapter to chapter so that the child will have experiences that range from art to cooking to manipulating objects. Read all the materials, the directions, and words of caution for every activity. All of the activities require *direct* adult supervision because of the materials used (such as scissors) or the nature of the activity (for example, cooking). Also be sure to clean your hands and your work area before and after doing these projects.

Discuss each activity with your child. Talk with the child while he or she is working on a particular project. Be patient, and praise the child as he or she is doing an activity. You may also find it helpful to repeat an activity. The projects are designed so that they can be enjoyed again. Here is a brief explanation of all the chapters:

For Starters. With these activities, children reinforce their command of beginning letter sounds and listening skills.

In Print. Here, the child learns to recognize printed letters.

Hands-On Fun. With these activities, the child learns letter recognition and also develops the small-muscle coordination necessary for writing.

See Words. With these activities, many of which are challenging, children apply their knowledge of letter sounds and recognition to beginning reading.

ABC Cook-Off. With the activities in this chapter, children will learn letter sounds while doing two of their favorite things—cooking and eating.

Crafty Sounds and Looks. Here, the child uses art materials to explore sounds and letters.

Word Play. The exciting phonics activities in this chapter will help the child learn letter sounds and word recognition while being active.

Most of all, have fun with the activities. The more enjoyable the phonics activities are for children, the more they'll want to do them— and the faster they'll learn to read.

FOR STARTERS

WHAT IS MISSING?

What You'll Need: Tray of items with different beginning sounds

Try this activity to enhance a child's visual awareness and beginning sound recognition.

On a tray, place a collection of five various items, each beginning with a different letter (for example, boat, pencil, apple, cup, and sock). Show the child the tray of items, and name them aloud. Then ask the child to turn around so he or she cannot see the tray. Remove one of the items, and place it behind your back. Have the child turn around. Ask the child to identify the missing item. Give a clue by telling the child that the missing item begins with a certain letter (for example, *S* for socks).

To make this activity more challenging, you can start with more objects; for younger children, you can start with as few as three objects. Reverse roles, and have the child remove an item from the tray. Ask him or her to give you a clue by telling you the beginning letter of the missing item.

ANIMAL SOUNDS

Exposing a child to the sounds that animals make is another way for him or her to be able to identify the sounds of different letters.

Make a sound that an animal makes, such as "moo." Ask the child to tell you the first letter of that sound. Continue with other animal sounds, having the child identify the beginning letter of each one. Reverse roles. Other sounds you can use: tweet, meow, baa, hee-haw, and woof.

Variation: Sing "Old MacDonald Had a Farm" to reinforce the animal sounds. If you have any interactive books that have recorded animal sounds, you can play those with the child as well.

PHONICS FUN FACT

Many animals use language to communicate with each other. For example, gorillas make noises to indicate that they are happy or to frighten another animal away. Some gorillas have even been taught American Sign Language so they can "talk" to humans.

PHONICS GO FISH

What You'll Need: Old magazines, blunt scissors, 10 or more index cards, glue or clear tape

The card game go fish is ideal for identifying words with the same beginning sounds.

Cut 10 or more pictures from magazines, and attach each one to an index card. Each picture name should have the same beginning sound as another picture name; for example, *bed/boy, cookie/car, lamp/lake, house/horse, roof/refrigerator.*

Shuffle the cards, then deal five cards to the child and five to yourself. First, lay down any pairs with matching sounds that either of you have. Then take turns asking each other for a card that will make a pair when combined with a card you already have. For example, "Do you have a picture whose name begins like *boy?*"

PHONICS FUN FACT

The letters *c* and *g* are different from some other consonants because they can spell more than one sound. The sound of *c* in *cat* is called a hard *c,* and the sound of *c* in *cent* is called a soft *c.* The sound of *g* in *goose* is called a hard *g.* The sound of *g* in *giraffe* is a soft *g.*

TONGUE TWISTER TIME

Many children have tried the tongue twister "Peter Piper picked a peck of pickled peppers." In this activity, let the child have fun with alliteration (two or more words in a row that begin with the same letter sound) and develop a new tongue twister.

It can be challenging to think of a sentence (or phrase) with words that all have the same beginning sound. ABC books, poetry books, and picture books that focus on alliteration can be read to the child. This is an enjoyable exercise and serves as a model.

After the child has developed his or her own tongue twister, see how fast it can be said by both the child and you. Then, test it with the rest of the family.

She sells seashells by the seashore.

Peter Piper picked a peck of pickled peppers!

WASH-DAY WORDS

What You'll Need: Clean laundry

Make helping out around the house a game of matching beginning sounds. As you and the child fold and sort clean laundry, have the child name each item and then say another word that begins with the same sound: for example, *socks/sun, jeans/jump,* or *towel/toy.*

A CLOSE LOOK

What You'll Need: Detailed ABC picture books

A beginning reader needs to develop the skill of observing and interpreting pictures. ABC books can help because they have illustrations that aid the child's understanding of the relationship between letters and their sounds. Some pages have one word, some have rhyming text, and some use alliteration (two or more words in a row that begin with the same letter sound). These books are useful because they help develop the foundations of phonics. At the same time, they are visually stimulating, helping to maintain the child's attention.

Examine a variety of ABC picture books, then ask the child to take a close look at one of them. Encourage the child to observe as much detail as possible. Next, select just one page, and say the word for an item depicted there. The child then needs to find something else on that page that begins with the same letter as the word you said. Alternate turns, paying attention to the letters and sounds as you go through the letters from *A* to *Z*.

I SPY

Play this game by giving clues that include beginning sounds. For example: "I spy something white. It is in the kitchen. It begins like the word *rabbit*." After the child answers correctly (refrigerator), give clues for another object.

LETTER RIDDLES

While traveling, shopping, or during spare time, play a riddle game that begins, for example, by saying, "I am thinking of the letter that has the beginning sound of *ball*. What letter is it?"

This activity provides many opportunities for riddles. A more challenging approach to the riddle concept is to present a series of clues. For example: "I am thinking of something that begins with a *B*." Allow the child to guess the answer between each successive clue. Continue with more clues: "I am thinking of something that is round. I am thinking of something that goes up very high and may be different colors. I am thinking of something that bounces."

Keep giving clues until the child guesses the object in mind. For a further variation, reverse roles and have the child give the clues. This activity helps develop the child's thinking skills as you progress from general to specific clues.

SOUND SORT

What You'll Need: Old magazines, blunt scissors, two shoe boxes, tape

Sorting pictures can help children practice identifying letter sounds.

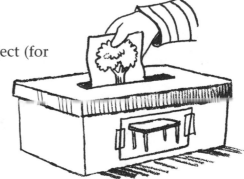

Cut pictures of objects out of old magazines. Tape a picture of an object (for example, a table) on the front of one of the shoe boxes. Have the child look through the other pictures you have cut out. Then the child can put into the box the pictures whose names begin with the same sound as the word *table*. Then change the picture on the first box, and tape a picture on the second box. Have the child sort through the pictures again, putting them into the two boxes according to beginning sounds.

This activity will work best if you find three or more pictures of things that begin with the same letter. For a variation, have the child sort actual objects.

SILLY WILLY

Young children get enjoyment from listening to and making up nonsense rhymes.

Begin by giving the child a word, such as *tall*. Ask him or her to think of a rhyming word, such as *ball*. Continue, alternating back and forth with who suggests the first word for silly rhyming. Some other words to begin the rhyming fun include *bat, hand, fox, tie, shoe, may,* and *tin*. Even though the word pairs you create may not always make sense, it is important that the child recognizes and responds to the rhyming concept.

PHONICS FUN FACT
The *Mother Goose* collection contains very famous nursery rhymes. These rhymes were first published in English in 1729.

ALPHABET TRAIN

What You'll Need: Boxes of various sizes and shapes, scissors, yarn, markers, objects beginning with the different letters of the alphabet

If possible, collect 26 small boxes and one larger box. Leave the open side of each box facing up. Line up the boxes end to end, like the boxcars of a train, then carefully cut a hole in the center of the front and back end of each "car." Use yarn to thread through the holes to connect the boxes. Make a knot on each end of the piece of yarn so that the yarn will not slip out.

When all 26 "cars" and one "engine" (the bigger box) are hooked together, write the alphabet on each of the small boxes—one letter per box in alphabetical order. When the train is assembled, ask the child to find some object that begins with each letter and place it in the appropriate "car."

Variation: If you can't find enough boxes, you can assign two or more letters per box.

PHONICS FUN FACT
The very first alphabet is thought to have originated between 1700 and 1500 B.C.

ABC—WHAT DO YOU SEE?

Children enjoy solving riddles, and this activity will help a child become aware of objects in the environment through riddles.

This game may be played in the home or anywhere. Begin by saying: "ABC, what do you see? I see something beginning with *T*." Have the child solve the riddle by saying something that he or she sees beginning with the letter *T* (for example, *table, teaspoon, tree*). You can give additional clues as needed, such as color, size, shape, function, or location. You can also ask the child to touch the object that he or she identifies. Reverse roles, and have the child choose a letter and start the riddle.

HIDDEN HANDS

What You'll Need: Box, collection of objects to feel, scissors

The five senses play a vital role in the life of a child. In this activity, the sense of touch is used.

To introduce this activity, show the child five objects (for example, apple, ball, feather, ribbon, and sock), and have the child say what the objects are. After the objects are properly identified, cut a hole in the box that is large enough for the child's hand to fit through. Place the objects inside the box. Then ask the child to reach inside, grasp an object, and describe what he or she is holding, then identify the beginning letter sound of the object.

Variation: Place five objects in the box without showing them to the child. Then ask him or her to feel, describe, name, and identify the beginning letter sounds of the objects.

WASH, RINSE, DRY

What You'll Need: Bathtub, water, washcloth, soap, towel

At bath time, try this beginning-sound chanting game.

Start with the word *wash.* As the child washes each arm, each leg, torso, and face with soap and cloth, he or she chants, "w-w-wash my arms, w-w-wash my legs," and so on for each body part. Repeat the activity with the word *rinse* ("r-r-rinse") as the child rinses each body part. Finally, use the word *dry* ("dr-dr-dry") as the child dries each body part.

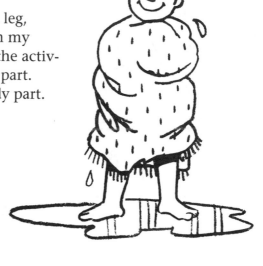

PHONICS FUN FACT

When two or more consonant sounds blend together, you can still hear all the consonant sounds. But the sounds together are a little different from each sound alone. Say the words *pay, lay,* and *play.* The blended sound at the beginning of *play* is made up of the *p* sound and the *l* sound, but as you can tell, the blended sound is different than both individual sounds. Some other blended sounds are *br, cl,* and *str.*

IN PRINT

SMALL, TALL, OR TAIL

What You'll Need: 26 letter cards, each showing one lowercase letter of the alphabet (and lined to show where the letter sits in relation to its baseline)

Categorizing lowercase letters will help the child learn and recall these letters.

Spread the lowercase letter cards on the floor or table. Pick out an example of a "small" letter (such as *a*), a "tall" letter (such as *b*), and a "tail" letter (one that goes below the baseline, such as *g*). Use these letters to start three piles. Have the child place all of the other letters into one of those three piles.

When the child is finished, the "small" pile should contain the letters *a, c, e, i, m, n, o, r, s, u, v, w, x,* and *z.* The "tall" pile should contain the letters *b, d, f, h, k, l,* and *t.* The "tail" pile should have the letters *g, j, p, q,* and *y.*

ALPHABET ACTIVITY BOOK

What You'll Need: Letter cards, hole punch, 18 inches of yarn, markers or crayons

Help the child create an alphabet book. Begin by punching one or two holes in each letter card and using the yarn to tie the cards together in order. Go through the letter book, and have the child suggest an activity for each letter; for example, *A* (*ask* a question), *B* (*bat* a ball), *C* (*cook* a meal), *D* (*dig* a hole). Suggest that the child draw and color a picture to illustrate each activity. Later, the child can choose a page and perform the activity.

ABC FLIPS

What You'll Need: Index cards, marker, lowercase letter cards

Capital letters are the first set of letters that a child learns. Capital letters serve as the point of reference in this activity, which is intended to help the child learn lowercase letters.

To make a flip card, take a 3×5-inch index card and fold it in half so the card stands up. On the exposed surface, write a capital letter. Write the matching lowercase letter on the inside half behind the capital letter flap.

Stand up the flip cards so the child can see all of the capital letters. Give the child the lowercase letter cards one letter at a time, and have him or her place each card by the matching capital letter on the flip card. The child can lift the flap to see if the lowercase letter matches the one that he or she selected.

TWO OF A KIND

What You'll Need: Paper, pen

Here's a simple activity that helps children practice seeing likenesses and differences between letters but does not require letter identification.

Write a row of letters on a sheet of paper. Write a few letters more than once. For example: C, E, C, D. Point to each letter, and ask the child to describe it. When you point to the letter C, the child might say, "It looks like a circle with an opening." Then have the child point to any two letters that are alike.

CHECKING LICENSE PLATES

What You'll Need: Paper, pencil

To pass the time when traveling in the car, give the child a sheet of paper with the alphabet printed on it in capital letters.

Have the child call out the letters that he or she sees on the license plates of other cars and then cross off those letters on the sheet of paper. Travel time will go by quickly when the child is involved with this activity, and he or she will be exposed to reading mixed combinations of letters and numbers.

WOODEN ALPHABET BLOCKS

What You'll Need: Wooden alphabet blocks

Give the child a set of alphabet blocks, and ask him or her to arrange the blocks in alphabetical order. As the blocks are being arranged, have the child say each letter.

Variation: On the blocks that have pictures, the child can match the corresponding letter block to that picture block.

PHONICS FUN FACT
The dictionary organizes words in alphabetical order. One of the first editors of an American English dictionary was Noah Webster. Way back in the 1850s, his spelling book sold more than a million copies annually. That's really amazing considering there were fewer than 23 million people in the United States then.

MUSICAL ALPHABET

What You'll Need: Letter cards, radio (or cassette or CD player)

The child's listening skills will get a workout in this activity.

Lay the letter cards in a big circle on the floor, spaced about one child's step apart.

Tell the child to walk around the outside of the circle, one step per letter, when the music starts playing. When the music stops, the child must stop and name a word that begins with the sound represented by the letter he or she is standing next to. Repeat until many different letters have been used.

PHONICS FUN FACT

Consonants and vowels can spell many sounds. Alone and together, consonants spell about 65 different sounds. That seems like a lot of sounds, but remember that there are 21 consonants. As opposed to consonants, the five vowels, alone and together, spell about 15 different sounds. And at least one of those vowel sounds occurs in every word in the English language.

ALPHABET STAMPS

What You'll Need: Stamp pad, alphabet stamps, paper

In this activity, the child uses small muscles in the hand to hold an alphabet stamp and print letters while learning letter recognition.

Get a stamp pad. Have the child take an alphabet stamp, press it onto the pad, and stamp the letter onto the paper to make a print of the letter. As each letter is printed, ask the child what letter it is. Discuss the lines of the letter. Are they curved or straight, or does the letter have both?

Continue printing letters. Ask the child to try to spell his or her name or other simple words. Have the child read what he or she has printed.

SEEK AND SAY

What You'll Need: Objects to hide, letter cards

Children love finding hidden objects. In this game, they will find objects and identify the beginning sounds of the objects' names.

Lay the letter cards out in rows. Hide objects, such as a variety of toys (ball, doll, teddy bear, car, top, jack-in-the-box, bat), around the room or yard. Have the child search for the toys. After finding a toy, he or she must locate the letter card that stands for the beginning sound in the toy's name in order to keep the card. Continue until all the objects are found and the beginning sounds of their names are identified. This is an especially good game for a group of children.

WORDS LIKE MY NAME

What You'll Need: Old magazines, blunt scissors, sheet of paper, glue or clear tape

Have the child become aware of words that begin with the same letter as his or her first and/or last name.

Give the child blunt scissors and some old magazines (those with a lot of advertisements and big print will work best). Talk about the first letter in his or her name, and start the search for words in the magazine beginning with that same letter. After the words are found and cut out, they may be glued or taped on paper. Read aloud the words that were chosen. Keep emphasizing that the words also have the same beginning letter as the child's name.

NEWSPAPER LETTERS

What You'll Need: Newspaper page, marker

This activity exposes the child to a newspaper, a medium in which letters and words are important.

Give the child a page from a newspaper, and ask him or her to search for a particular letter. Every time that letter is found, have the child put a circle around it with a marker. You may limit this to capital or lowercase letters, or search for both. Try different letters, and have the child note the frequency of some letters (such as *E*) compared to others (for example, *X*).

CARD CLAP

What You'll Need: Two matching sets of letter cards

Use letter cards for this letter-recognition game. Begin by using only the *A* through *M* cards of both sets. Shuffle each set of cards. Place the two sets in side-by-side piles.

Pick up and display the top card of each set. Tell the child to clap if the two cards show the same letter, in which case put the matching cards aside. If the two cards do not match, place each one at the bottom of its pile. Continue until all matching pairs have been identified. Then put the cards back into their sets, shuffle each set, and repeat the activity. Add new matching pairs of cards to the sets when the child has mastered the first half of the alphabet.

SCRAMBLED LETTERS

What You'll Need: Three clean egg cartons, scissors, marker, construction paper, small container

Sorting letters into egg cartons is one way to recognize letter likenesses and differences.

Cut off the tops of the egg cartons so that you have three bottoms with 12 hollow sections each. With a marker, print a letter on the bottom of each section, with *A* to *I* in the first carton, *J* to *R* in the second carton, and *S* to *Z* in the third carton. Using construction paper, cut out 26 circles approximately one inch in diameter and print one letter of the alphabet on each one. Put the letter discs in a small container, and mix them. Have the child take out the discs one at a time and put each into its matching egg-carton section.

SPIDER MAN

What You'll Need: Cotton balls, 18- to 24-inch length of yarn, blunt scissors, clear tape, construction paper, marker, glue, poster board or butcher paper

Invite children to play a board game that uses their ability to recognize like and different letters.

First, make a spider game piece for each player. Use a cotton ball for each spider's body. Cut and tape eight short pieces of yarn to the bottom of the cotton ball for legs. Draw, cut, and glue two construction-paper eyes on the top of the cotton ball. For the game board, draw a path of squares on the poster board or a sheet of butcher paper. At the end of the path, draw a spiderweb. In each square, write a pair of capital letters, sometimes the same (*B, B*) and sometimes different (*E, F*). Players take turns moving a spider to each square on the path and telling whether the letters on the square are the same or different.

LETTER ORDER

What You'll Need: Set of letter cards with capital letters, set of letter cards with lowercase letters

Children can manipulate letter cards to learn alphabetical order.

Remove the capital letter cards *A* through *F* from the first set of cards. Mix the six cards. Ask the child to lay the cards out in alphabetical order. When he or she is ready for more challenging activities, use additional capital letters and then lowercase letters.

ALPHABET HUNT

What You'll Need: Letter cards, legal pad or clipboard, marker or pen

Here's a great way to brush up on all of the letters in the alphabet.

Remove any one letter card from a complete set of letter cards representing the entire alphabet. Place the remaining 25 cards around a room in plain sight, but in random order, then help the child write the letters of the alphabet in proper order down the page on a legal pad.

Instruct the child to go around the room and put a check mark on the pad beside the appropriate letter as he or she finds each card. When the child has finished this task, ask him or her to identify the letter on the pad that does not have a check mark. For beginners, use only the first 10 letters of the alphabet.

PHONICS FUN FACT

Some people believe the first words were written around 6000 B.C. It is generally agreed that writing tries to symbolize the sounds of languages.

FISHING FOR LETTERS

What You'll Need: Construction paper; blunt scissors; marker or pen; paper clips; dowel rod; string; magnet; bathtub, dish pan, or inflatable swimming pool (optional)

Here is an opportunity for a child to go fishing—for letters.

Using several sheets of construction paper, cut out 26 fish shapes. Write one letter of the alphabet in uppercase and lowercase on both sides of each fish. Affix a paper clip to each fish. To make the fishing pole, take a dowel rod and tie a piece of string onto one end. At the end of the string, tie a magnet. To set the atmosphere for this activity, you could place the paper fish in a bathtub, dish pan, or inflatable swimming pool. (They should not contain water.)

The task for the child is to use the fishing pole to catch a fish. The magnet will attract the paper clip on each fish. When a fish is caught, have the child pull it gently off the magnet and say the letter.

PHONICS FUN FACT
Letters *I, T, L,* and *X* are the easiest letters to write.

ALPHABET NITTY GRITTY

What You'll Need: Sandpaper, blunt scissors

Some children learn better through activities that concentrate on touch. Cut letter shapes out of sandpaper. Invite the child to trace each letter with his or her finger while saying which letter it is.

MATCH ME

What You'll Need: Several children's magazines, letter cards (capital letters), blunt scissors

A subscription to a children's magazine can be very exciting for him or her. He or she may come to anticipate each issue and the opportunity to learn new things.

Save back issues of any children's magazines. Ask the child to find a lowercase letter in the magazine that matches each capital letter on the letter cards, which you randomly present to him or her one card at a time. As each letter is found, the child cuts it out and places it on the letter card next to its corresponding capital.

HANDS–ON FUN

CLOUD PICTURES

What You'll Need: White chalk or crayon, blue construction paper

Looking for images in cloud formations is a great creative exercise. With a little extra effort, you can also turn it into a lesson in beginning letters.

On a day with many clouds in the sky, go outside with the child and talk about the clouds, noting how they sometimes look like animals or objects. Take turns pointing out clouds and saying what you think they resemble.

While outside or when you get back inside, ask the child to re-create some of the cloud objects he or she saw by drawing them with white chalk or crayon on blue construction paper. Encourage the child to describe the cloud drawings to you, then print the beginning letter of the object that the cloud resembles in the upper-right corner of the page.

PICTURE THIS

What You'll Need: Detailed "action" picture, paper, marker or pen

As a child learns to read, interpreting pictures becomes a big part of the language process.

In this activity, the child is asked to look very closely at a detailed action picture and describe what he or she sees. A child who cannot read will name specific objects that are seen—for example, a ball, a girl, a flower. A beginning reader is often able to describe what he or she sees with greater detail. As the child is telling you what object he or she sees, ask him or her what the beginning letter is. Then write the word down for the child to see.

LETTER FEELINGS

What You'll Need: Magnetic or wooden capital and/or lowercase letters, bag

This activity focuses the child's attention on the formation of letters, which is necessary for letter recognition.

Place all the capital or lowercase letters in a bag. Have the child reach inside the bag, feel a letter, and describe it so that you can guess what letter it is (for example, the letter *A* might be described as two long diagonal lines with a smaller line between them). Then reverse roles. You pick and describe a letter, and the child tries to guess its identity.

REPTILE FAMILY

What You'll Need: Construction paper, pen or marker, blunt scissors, plastic container

Here's a personalized puzzle that helps children recognize several kinds of likenesses and differences.

Make several snakes by drawing and cutting out squiggly snake shapes from different colors of construction paper. Along each snake, write the name of a family member or friend in large letters with space between the letters. Cut each snake into pieces with a letter on each piece. Put all the pieces into a container, and mix them. Have the child put each snake back together by matching colors, letters, and edges.

PHONICS FUN FACT

A consonant *digraph* is a pair of consonants that spells one sound, not two. This sound is usually different from the sound that either letter spells on its own. Listen to the beginning sound in *chair:* It's not the *k* sound or the *s* sound that *c* usually spells. And it's not the *h* sound that *h* usually spells.

MACARONI LETTERS

What You'll Need: 18-inch length of yarn, uncooked macaroni

Tasks such as threading pieces of macaroni on a string can help a child improve hand-eye coordination, which is necessary for learning to read and write.

Tie a knot at the end of a length of yarn, and show the child how to string macaroni on it. When the string of macaroni is complete, tie a knot at the other end. Ask the child to make different letters by laying the string of macaroni on a tabletop and forming letter shapes.

COMPUTER COPYCAT

What You'll Need: Computer, pencil, sheet of paper

Expose a child to a device he or she will have to master someday—the computer keyboard—while he or she practices identifying and copying letters.

Show the child where letters are located on a computer keyboard. Press the "caps lock" key so that only capital letters will be displayed. Tell the child to press any letter key, then have him or her copy the letter with a pencil on a sheet of paper.

Continue by having the child press as many as five letter keys, copying the series of letters on paper. More advanced children can be directed to press specific letters to spell a word they know.

ALPHABET QUILT

What You'll Need: Two sheets of poster board, marker or pen, ruler, sheet of paper, quilt picture in book or magazine (optional), blunt scissors, crayons or colored pencils

Because making an alphabet quilt takes time, finishing one gives a child a real sense of accomplishment. Besides reinforcing letter recognition, this activity gives a child a strong introduction to two-dimensional letters.

Draw lines to divide one sheet of poster board into 30 squares. Then write the letter Q and the word *quilt* on a sheet of paper. Explain that a real quilt is made of cloth; display one if available, or find a picture of one in a book or magazine. Point out that quilts have interesting patterns that are sewn on.

Tell the child that he or she will make an alphabet pattern on paper that can be used to make a cloth quilt. On another poster board, draw and cut out a pattern for each letter of the alphabet sized to fit inside the quilt squares. (Since the alphabet has only 26 letters, repeat any four letters, draw designs, or leave blanks in the 4 corners.) Instruct the child to trace the letter patterns within the quilt squares and then color them. This can be an ongoing project if you do a few letters each day.

READ TO ME

What You'll Need: Children's picture books

Pretending to read helps children prepare to do the real thing.

Ask the child to read you a book. Read the title together. Then show the child how to turn the pages from the beginning to the end of the book. Encourage the child to tell you the story in the book by looking at the pictures. Ask him or her to find two words that look alike. Say the two words to the child, pointing out letters that are the same.

CHENILLE STEM LETTERS

What You'll Need: Chenille stems

Children love to twist and bend chenille stems. The challenge in this activity is to make capital and lowercase letters with them.

Initially, give the child four chenille stems. The child will need to think of the type and number of lines that are needed to make a particular letter. For example, the letter *M* has four straight lines (two vertical and two diagonal), while the letter *S* is one continuous curved line. Have fun and see if the child can spell his or her name using chenille stems.

Variation: For a challenge, see if the child can use only one chenille stem to make a letter.

CHAIN OF LETTERS

What You'll Need: Construction paper, blunt scissors, glue, letter cards

In this activity, the child creates a long paper chain, which he or she can use to form any of the alphabet's letters.

Cut several strips of paper approximately 6 inches long. Help the child make a paper chain by gluing the first strip into a circle and then linking and gluing the strips inside one another to make a chain. When the chain is about 24 inches long, ask the child to lay the chain down in the shapes of letters that he or she copies from letter cards.

WACKY WEEK

Use song and pantomime to practice beginning sounds in words. Sing an "action" song about the days of the week to the tune of "Here We Go 'Round the Mulberry Bush." For example:

This is the way we wash our windows,

Wash our windows, wash our windows,

This is the way we wash our windows

So early Wednesday morning.

Have the child think of an action using words that begin with the same letter as the name of each day of the week. For example, "munch our meat on Monday" and "tickle a tiger on Tuesday." Encourage the child to pantomime each action as he or she sings the song.

WALKING THE TIGHTROPE

What You'll Need: Rope cut in 4-inch lengths

The challenge of walking a tightrope is exciting to a child. The motor skills necessary for balancing have to be used in this activity.

Take a piece (or pieces) of rope, and outline a very large letter (capital or lower-case) on the floor. The goal of this activity is for the child to "tightrope-walk" this letter. Make sure that, as the child is walking this letter, he or she is moving in the way that the letter is properly formed (top to bottom and left to right). Also, arms can be extended sideways to simulate the moves of a tightrope walker.

Variation: For an additional challenge, the child can walk sideways, moving one foot next to the other, or the child can be asked to cross one foot over the other.

PHONICS FUN FACT

The printing press, invented around 1450, made more copies of a book available. Prior to this, every book had to be recorded and copied by hand.

SEE WORDS

ME WORDS

Cute Adorable Terrific Happy Interesting

What You'll Need: Paper, marker or pen

This activity helps expand a child's vocabulary and grasp of beginning word sounds.

Ask the child to think of a word beginning with each letter of his or her first name. Tell the child that each word should be one that describes him or her. Using the name Cathi as an example, the child might pick the words *Cute, Adorable, Terrific, Happy,* and *Interesting.*

It can be entertaining to hear the words a child will use to describe himself or herself.

PHONICS FUN FACT
If you were to hear someone from a really long time ago—for example, from the year 900—speak in English, it would sound like a foreign language.

TIC-TAC-TOE RHYMES

What You'll Need: Two sheets of drawing paper, marker or pen, crayons or coloring pencils, blunt scissors, board game markers

Here's a way to play this classic game while learning to recognize letters and rhyming words.

Make a game card by dividing a sheet of drawing paper into nine squares (three rows of three squares). Help the child draw or color the following pictures inside the squares: a hat, mouse, boy, peach, car, goose, tree, boat, and dime. Divide a second sheet of paper into nine squares. This time, the child should draw or color a cat, house, toy, beach, jar, moose, bee, coat, and lime inside the squares and then cut this second set of squares apart with blunt scissors.

To play, shuffle the picture cards. Players take turns picking a card and matching it to a rhyming word on the game board. If a player makes a correct match, he or she puts a board game marker on the square. The first player to get three markers across, down, or on a diagonal wins the game.

PHONICS FUN FACT

Poetry doesn't always have to rhyme. However, from around 1300 to the end of the 1500s, only rhyming poetry was considered outstanding. Around the year 1600, poetry that didn't rhyme, called blank verse, was introduced.

WORD SHOPPING

What You'll Need: Index cards, plastic or paper grocery bag, marker or pen

Familiar food names are a good starting place for learning to read words.

Using index cards, make word cards with food names such as *apple, cookie, meat, milk,* and *juice.* Have the child choose a card, and say the word together. Then invite the child to go grocery shopping. To "buy" a card and put it in the bag, the child must say the food name on the card.

Variation: You might also use toy food items or even real fruits and vegetables with the word cards.

WORDS ON THE GO

What You'll Need: Paper, pencil

Reading takes place not only at home and school but also elsewhere within one's environment.

Make a long trip seem shorter by giving the child a piece of paper and a pencil. Whenever the child sees a word or sign that he or she can read, have him or her say the word and write it down on the paper. For example: *stop, do, not, gas, turn, go.* At the end of the trip, tally how many words were recognized. Ask the child to read the list of words aloud.

REFRIGERATOR WORDS

What You'll Need: Magnetic letters, index cards, pen or marker

While you are in the kitchen preparing dinner, the child can be with you constructing words on the refrigerator with magnetic letters.

Buy a set of magnetic letters, and give the child a word card (an index card with, for example, the word *dog* printed on it). Have him or her find the matching magnetic letters to spell the word. Direct the child to place each magnetic letter on the refrigerator door. Have him or her say each letter and make its sound. When all the letters of the word are placed together, have the child put those sounds together to say the word.

Repeat the activity with other words. It will be fun to share this time together in the kitchen.

WORD FACTORY

What You'll Need: 36 blank index cards, marker or pen

Play a game that challenges a child to put letters together to make words.

Make a letter card for each letter of the alphabet. Make two extra sets of the letters *A, E, I, O,* and *U.* Give each player six cards (make sure at least one of the cards is a vowel). Work with the child to create words using as many of the six letters as possible. Have the players take turns making words. After spelling a word, a player may replace the used cards with new cards.

WEATHER CHART

What You'll Need: Construction paper of various colors to make weather symbols (for example, yellow to make a sun, white to make clouds, blue for raindrops), blunt scissors, monthly calendar (with the days of the week spelled out)

Children are curious about the weather: What makes it rain? Why is it sunny?

Help the child to make an assortment of weather symbols—a sun, clouds, raindrops, etc. Each day, he or she can place the appropriate weather symbol on the calendar square for that day. Have the child go outside or look out the window and observe the weather conditions. Is it sunny, rainy, or snowy? Discuss the weather each day, then let the child select the appropriate weather symbol.

By using a calendar every day, the child will learn to recognize and read the days of the week. He or she will also learn how symbols represent words.

KNOCK-KNOCK!

What You'll Need: Index cards, marker or pen

In this game, children have to give a nonverbal signal to indicate whether words they are shown are alike or different.

Make a set of word cards with simple words. Make duplicate word cards for about half the words. Explain to the child that you will play a game in which one knock signals "yes" and two knocks signal "no." Tell the child to knock on the table once to signal "yes" if you show two words that are alike and knock twice to signal "no" if they are not alike. Then show the child two word cards at a time.

COLOR COORDINATES

What You'll Need: Crayons, index cards

Children can learn to recognize color words as they work on beginning sounds.

Make word cards with the color words *red, orange, pink, tan,* and *violet.* Lay out the word cards, along with crayons representing each of the colors, in random order. Say, "I see a color that starts like the word *very*," and have the child choose the word card and crayon that apply. (Answer: violet.) Continue with the other colors.

FREQUENT WORD SEARCH

What You'll Need: Word cards, crayons, magazine page with words

What words are used most frequently? This is the time for the child to find out.

Think of a word that you believe is used frequently (for example, *the*). Give the child a card with that word on it, a crayon, and a magazine page. Every time the child sees that word on the magazine page, he or she is to put a circle around it. Search the entire page. When finished, count how many times that word was used. Remind the child that the word might begin with a capital letter.

Choose another word (for example, *on*). Give the child the word card, and using a different crayon, have him or her circle that word on the magazine page. Then count and tally. See which word was used more frequently. Try searching for and counting words that the child thinks are used a lot.

LITTLE WORD SEARCH

What You'll Need: Paper, pen

In this activity, children learn reading skills by recognizing a small word in a longer word.

Write a row of words. Start with a small word, and then write two longer words that contain the small word. Ask the child to underline the "little" word in each longer word, then tell how the longer words are different. Encourage advanced children to read as many words as possible. Start with the following word rows:

up pup puppy
an and hand
it bit bite
jump jumped jumping
play plays replay

PHONE FUN

What You'll Need: Telephone, word cards

Children will feel like a grown-up when they make a telephone call to share their word skills with a friend or relative.

Review a set of word cards that the child has learned. Help the child call a favorite adult friend or relative on the telephone and read the words that he or she knows. Prepare the adult ahead of time so that he or she offers plenty of praise and encouragement.

RHYMING CIRCLES

What You'll Need: Lightweight cardboard, ruler, blunt scissors, marker or pen, brad fastener

The child will be able to learn and review new rhyming words with this activity.

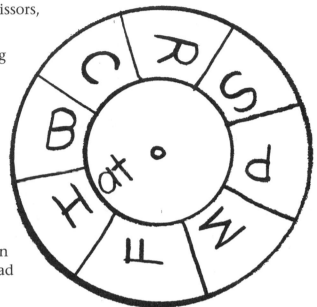

Cut a circle measuring approximately 8 inches in diameter from a sheet of lightweight cardboard. With a marker or pen, divide the circle into eight equal segments, as if it were a pie. At the outer edge of the circle, write a different, frequently used consonant (for example, *S, P, T, C,* etc.) in each segment. Make eight 3-inch diameter circles, and on each circle write one of the following letter pairs: *at, an, in, on, un, ap, op.* Put a hole in the center of each circle. Place one of the smaller circles on top of the 8-inch circle. Connect the two circles with a brad fastener.

Have the child turn the big circle and line up the different consonants with the letter pair on the smaller circle. See what words can be created by doing this. Note, however, that not all of the combinations work. Point this out to the child. Try new centers for new words.

PHONICS FUN FACT
Up until the end of the fifteenth century, people spelled English words pretty much any way they wished. They even made up their own spellings!

BODY LANGUAGE

What You'll Need: Index cards, marker or pen,

Here's a phonics activity that also tests a child's quickness and coordination.

Write the words *head, neck, leg, foot,* and *toe* on separate index cards. Read each card with the child. Have the child identify the beginning sound in each word and touch the body part the word names. Shuffle the cards, and place them facedown. Instruct the child to choose one card at a time, identify the body part named on the card, touch that body part, and then say another word with the same beginning sound. Remind the child to identify the initial sound in both words.

 # SPINNING WHEEL

What You'll Need: Construction paper, pen or pencil, small piece of poster board, blunt scissors, paper fastener

Children can use pictures to learn to read the words for their favorite toys.

On a sheet of construction paper, draw a large circle, and divide it into six or eight sections. Ask the child to name several favorite toys. Write one of the toy names in each section of the circle. Have the child draw a picture in each section that matches the word.

Meanwhile, make a spinner out of poster board. Attach it to the center of the circle with a paper fastener. Take turns spinning the spinner and reading the word in the section in which the spinner stops. When the child has mastered the toy words, make circles for animal words, food words, and so on.

ZOO

What You'll Need: Sheet of paper, marker or pen

Children's natural love of animals can be channeled into wordplay that helps develop reading skills.

On a sheet of paper, print the word *ZOO* in capital letters. Ask the child to identify the first letter of the word. Say the word together several times.

Talk with the child about trips to the zoo, or discuss zoos he or she may have seen on TV or in movies. Encourage the child to think about some of the animals he or she saw there. Whenever the child mentions a specific animal, ask him or her to identify the beginning letter of the animal's name. Make a list of all the animals the child names, then show him or her the list and say, "Can you find the ____?" Read one of the animal names on the list, and see if the child can find that word.

Variation: Take turns acting like zoo animals, such as an elephant, monkey, gorilla, lion, and bear, as the other player guesses the animal's identity and identifies the word on the list.

BUILD A WORD

What You'll Need: Index cards, marker or pen

Putting two cards together to make a word will help children understand word construction.

Make two sets of cards. One set has a card for each of the following consonants: *B, C, D, F, S.* The other set has a card for each of the following word endings:

at et it ob ut
an ell ip ot un

Lay the consonant cards on a table, and put the word-ending cards in a pile. Have the child take a word-ending card and put it next to each consonant card that the word ending can be combined with to make a word. Have the child read each word. Continue through the set of word-ending cards.

PHONICS FUN FACT
The first publications written just for children were meant to teach them. For example, the hornbook, invented in the 1400s, included the alphabet in both uppercase and lowercase letters. Some hornbooks even taught children numerals and prayers.

ABC COOK–OFF

COOKIE CORNER

What You'll Need: Cookie dough, rolling pin, letter cookie cutters, baking sheet, decorative icing in tubes

Children can learn about letters as they eat their favorite snack.

Ask the child to help you mix a batch of cookie dough. Cookie dough from a mix, frozen dough, or refrigerated rolls of dough all work well. Roll the dough out. Have the child use cookie cutters shaped like letters to cut the dough. After baking and cooling the cookies, help the child decorate each cookie by tracing the shape of each letter with decorative icing in a tube.

Put the cookie letters out on a plate. Play an easy game of I spy, taking turns giving clues, such as, "I spy a letter that begins the word *apple*." Each cookie letter may be eaten after it has been correctly identified.

PHONICS FUN FACT
Some African languages use click sounds. The click sounds are sometimes uttered at the same time as other sounds.

GELATIN ALPHABET

What You'll Need: Gelatin dessert mix (and listed ingredients), flat pan, letter cookie cutters, spatula, plate

In this game, children can learn their letters and eat them too!

Ask the child to help you make a gelatin dessert in any favorite flavor. Chill the gelatin in a long, flat pan. When it has solidified, use cookie cutters shaped like letters to make as many different letter shapes as possible. Use a spatula to pick up the letters, and put them on a plate. Have the child name each letter before eating it. Children with more advanced reading skills can arrange the letters to spell their names or another word before they eat the letters.

TOUCHABLE FRUIT SALAD

What You'll Need: Fruits as described below, scarf for blindfold, large bowl, knife, cutting board

Help a child master beginning letters while making a healthy snack that both of you can enjoy.

Collect as many of these fresh fruits as possible: apple, orange, grapes, pineapple, cantaloupe, peach, grapefruit, and banana. Have the child put on a blindfold, feel each fruit, and guess what it is. After each fruit is named correctly, take the blindfold off. Ask him or her to say another word that begins with the same sound as the name of the fruit.

Then ask the child to help you prepare each fruit for a fruit salad. Have the child do as many steps as is safely possible, such as washing fruit, peeling the banana, and pulling grapes from their stems. Discuss the other steps, such as cutting up the fruits, as you do them.

HAMBURGER HELPER

What You'll Need: Ground meat, buns, other items used to make a hamburger meal

Helping with a hamburger meal is a great way for children to learn not only the steps in meal preparation but beginning sounds in words as well.

Have the child help you prepare a meal of hamburgers, starting with making the patties. As the two of you work, discuss each food item you are using: meat, salt, pepper, bun, mustard, ketchup, pickles, beans, potato chips, and so on. Have the child name other words that begin with the same sound as the name of each food item. Using the word *meat,* for example, the child might respond with the words *map, man, mouse, make,* or *mind.*

PHONICS FUN FACT
When an *e* appears at the end of the word, it usually makes the vowel before it have a long sound, such as *cane, kite,* and *hope.*

ALPHABET NOODLES

What You'll Need: Box of alphabet noodles, bowl

When grocery shopping, go down the pasta aisle. Select a box of alphabet noodles. Many phonics activities can be done with them.

In this particular activity, empty the alphabet noodles into a bowl. Have the child group the noodles by letter (all of the *A*'s, *B*'s, *C*'s, and so on). When this task is completed, help the child determine whether any letters of the alphabet are missing, which letters are the most common, and so on.

GOING CRACKERS

What You'll Need: Box of animal crackers, paper, marker or pen

In this activity, children practice both sorting and identifying beginning sounds.

Have the child put animal crackers into groups according to kind of animal. Then ask him or her to identify each kind of animal and say the letter that stands for the beginning sound in its name. Have the child write each beginning letter on a sheet of paper, or write each letter yourself and have the child copy it. Finally, have the child place each animal cracker on the paper next to the beginning letter of its name.

PRETZEL PRACTICE

What You'll Need: Pretzel sticks

Not only are pretzels a tasty snack, but kids also can use them to form letters without making a mess.

Ask the child to wash his or her hands, then show him or her how to use pretzel sticks to form letters, including breaking them in half to form some letter parts. Start with simple stick letters such as *E, I,* and *T.* You might progress to making all the letters in the alphabet. Say each letter as the child makes it, and also have him or her name each letter frequently.

FLOUR POWER

What You'll Need: Cookie sheet, flour, paper, marker or pen

Use a common kitchen staple in a unique version of finger painting.

Spread flour on a cookie sheet so that the entire surface is covered with approximately ⅛ to ¼ inch of flour. Show the child how to print letters in the flour using an index finger. Then select one letter, and have the child write both the capital and lowercase forms of the letter (for example, *Bb*) in the flour. Have the child write the letters on paper and then draw pictures of items whose names begin with the letter (ball, bat, bird, bell, bed).

MINI-PIZZA RECIPE

What You'll Need: English muffins, baking sheet, tomato sauce, spoon, vegetable toppings (if desired), shredded mozzarella cheese, paper, crayons

Not sure what to make for lunch? How about mini-pizzas? Preheat your oven to 425 degrees, and place the ingredients on a table or counter.

First, split a muffin in half, and place the halves on a baking sheet. (You can toast the muffin first, if you want a crunchy crust.) Show the child how to spoon tomato sauce onto the muffins, followed by any vegetable toppings that he or she may like—onions and mushrooms, for example. Let the child put the cheese on the pizzas, then bake them for 10 to 15 minutes. As always, be careful that the child doesn't come into contact with the stove or heated baking pan.

While the pizzas are baking, help the child make a recipe card using pictures and beginning letters. Arrange them sequentially to show how the mini-pizzas were made. For example:

1. Picture of a muffin and the letter *M*.

2. Picture of sauce on a muffin half and the letter *S*.

3. Picture of vegetable toppings, if used, along with their beginning letters.

4. Picture of cheese and the letters *Ch*.

CRAFTY SOUNDS AND LOOKS

ANIMAL FINGERS

What You'll Need: Felt, blunt scissors, glue or clear tape, bits of yarn, markers or construction paper

Encourage children's dramatic talents by making finger puppets that they can use to act out animal characters.

Cut out two finger-shaped pieces of felt approximately 1×2 inches. Glue or tape them together along the edges so that the child's finger will fit into the pocket. Start with a cat character. Help the child glue or tape on bits of yarn for whiskers and a tail, and use markers or construction paper to make eyes and ears. Have the child put the puppet on a finger and name words that begin like *cat,* using a cat's "voice." Continue by making dog, bird, lamb, and tiger puppets.

LEFT OR RIGHT

What You'll Need: Red and blue tempera paint, paintbrush, white paper

A prerequisite for reading is to be able to differentiate between left and right, since the reading process requires a left-to-right progression. The concepts of left and right can be confusing for a child, but with a little help from painted hands, a memory association can be made.

Use a paintbrush to paint the palm of the child's right hand red. Emphasize the beginning sound of *right* and *red*. Then make an impression of that painted hand on a piece of white paper. Next, use blue paint to make a similar impression using the child's left palm. After the child's hands are washed and the handprints are dry, he or she can practice matching both hands to the prints. To further assist the child, a red ribbon may be tied around the right wrist, a blue ribbon around the left one.

PHONICS FUN FACT
Some languages are written from right to left instead of left to right like English. One example is Yiddish, which is spoken by around 5 million Jews all over the world.

FUN FOLDERS

What You'll Need: File folders, marker or pen, old magazines, blunt scissors, glue or clear tape

A file folder makes an excellent organizer for pictures illustrating beginning sounds.

Print the letters *Ff* on the front of a folder. Have the child look through magazines for pictures of objects whose names begin with the letter *F*. Cut out the pictures, and arrange them in an interesting layout across the middle of the opened folder. Glue or tape the pictures in place. You can make additional folders for other letters of the alphabet.

BUILDING BOXES

What You'll Need: Boxes of various sizes and shapes

Begin this activity by asking the child to think of different things that might be found in a box. Then see how many different boxes can be located in the home.

After several boxes are collected, ask the child to build something using these boxes as building blocks. Whatever the child constructs—a castle, tunnel, tower, house, or something else—ask him or her to identify the beginning letter of that structure. Ask the child what else he or she can build with the boxes.

VEGETABLE PRINTS

What You'll Need: Several clean foam food trays (only from fruits or vegetables), tempera paint, vegetables (such as pepper, mushroom, broccoli, cauliflower, radish, carrot, onion, and potato), knife, construction paper, marker

Vegetables such as peppers and onions have distinctive aromas. In addition, they have distinctive shapes and textures.

Pour some tempera paint onto several foam food trays. Show the child some vegetables, and see if he or she can identify them. Then ask, "What letter does the word *vegetables* begin with?" Cut portions of the vegetables so that the child can handle them.

Have the child select a cut vegetable, then tell you what it is and its beginning letter. Next, instruct the child to dip the cut vegetable into the paint and "print" it on the paper. Continue with different vegetables and paints.

When the prints are dry, ask the child, "What type of food beginning with the letter *V* was used to make all the prints?" Discuss the shapes and characteristics of each vegetable as the child points to its print and says its beginning letter. Have the child write that letter under each vegetable print with a marker.

SUN SHAPES

What You'll Need: Collection of familiar objects (such as a pencil, ruler, marker, and paper clip), dark-colored construction paper, marker or pen

This activity blends science and phonics.

On a sunny day, help the child collect some objects that are easily recognizable by their shapes—for example, a pencil, ruler, marker, and paper clip. Discuss the beginning letters and sounds of those objects.

Next, ask the child to select a piece of dark-colored construction paper. Then take the collected objects and the paper outside. Place the paper on the ground, in direct sunlight, and have the child arrange the objects on the paper. (You may need to place some heavy stones on the edges of the paper if it is a windy day.)

Approximately one hour later, instruct the child to remove the objects from the paper. Ask the child what he or she sees, and discuss what happened to the paper. As each image is identified, have him or her use a marker or pen to write the beginning letter under each image left under the object (*P* for pencil, *M* for marker, *R* for ruler, and so on).

PHONICS FUN FACT

The written languages of Chinese and Japanese don't use alphabets. Actually, even though the characters in both languages may look alike to you, they are quite different. Each Chinese character signifies a word or idea, while each Japanese character represents a syllable.

LETTER SELF-PORTRAIT

What You'll Need: Large sheet of heavy paper, crayons or markers

Do this project to personalize a child's study of letters.

Find a large sheet of paper that is sturdy and a few inches longer than the child's height. Put the paper on the floor, have the child lie on it, and trace around him or her. Have the child color the "self-portrait" with crayons or markers and print his or her name at the top.

Encourage the child to add distinguishing characteristics of dress, hairstyle, and so on. Write the first letter of the child's name, and have the child draw pictures of toys whose names begin with that letter.

WHERE DID THEY GO?

What You'll Need: Water, container, paintbrush

What happens on a sunny day when there's water on the sidewalk? Let the child find out.

On a bright, warm day, take the child outside. Give him or her a paintbrush and a container partly filled with water. Find a safe and sunny cement surface (such as the sidewalk), and have the child "paint" letters of the alphabet. The child will be amazed at how quickly the letters disappear.

WHAT CAN IT BE?

What You'll Need: Paper, crayons or markers

It's good to stimulate a child's creativity. Here's one great way to do it.

Draw a large letter (capital or lowercase) on a piece of paper. Ask the child to create an object based on the letter's shape (for example, the letter *O* can be made into a wheel, the letter *V* into an ice cream cone). Label the drawing. See how many objects the child can create with different letters. When the project is completed, show the drawings to other family members to see if they can find the letter.

SPONGE PAINTING

What You'll Need: Small sponges, paint, shallow dish, paper

Children will enjoy the patterns created by using a sponge as a painting tool.

To make the sponges, you can cut a new kitchen sponge into pieces approximately 1×2 inches. Put tempera paint, finger paint, or poster paint in a shallow dish. Show the child how to dip a sponge in the paint and stamp it on a sheet of paper. (Heavy art paper will work best, but any kind of paper will do.)

Next, show the child how to form a letter by making several stamps to form a letter shape. Encourage the child to make several letters, such as his or her name or the alphabet. The child may also wish to make a large letter and then draw pictures of objects whose names have that beginning sound.

BIG BUBBLES

What You'll Need: Plastic bowl, water, liquid detergent, food coloring, straws, white paper

To demonstrate comparison words and the sounds of word endings *er* and *est*, try making bubbles to show the concepts of big, bigger, and biggest.

Take a medium-size plastic bowl, and fill it three-fourths full with water. Add a small amount of liquid detergent and food coloring. Demonstrate the fine art of blowing bubbles by putting one end of a straw into the liquid and blowing gently into the other end. Then have the child try it.

Have the child blow a bubble, then a bigger bubble, and finally, the biggest bubble he or she can make. As the bubbles appear at the top of or over the container, take a piece of paper, put it over the container, and make an instant print of the bubble. If you use different colors or bubble mixtures, you can add those bubble prints to the same sheet of paper. When finished, look at the bubble prints with the child. Ask him or her to show you the big, bigger, and biggest bubbles.

PHONICS FUN FACT
There are more than 2,500 spoken languages in the world. The most widely spoken language is Chinese (Mandarin).

MONEY ART

What You'll Need: Penny, nickel, dime, quarter, crayons, thin or regular paper

The child will be using small hand muscles as he or she is making rubbings of different coins and learning about them at the same time.

Show the child a penny, nickel, dime, and quarter. Say, "I am thinking of a word that begins like *mouse* that describes all of these coins. What word is it?" (Answer: *money*.) Discuss with the child the colors and sizes of the coins. Ask, "What beginning letter sound do you hear in the words *penny, nickel, dime,* and *quarter?*" (P, N, D, and Q.)

Have the child select a crayon and a coin. Put a sheet of thin or regular paper over the coin, and instruct the child to rub the crayon over the paper where the coin is. This will create an imprint of the coin. Repeat this with the other coins. When all of the money has been rubbed, have the child match the coins to the coin imprints and write the beginning letter of each coin next to the corresponding crayon imprint.

PICTURE PLATES

What You'll Need: Old magazines, blunt scissors, small paper plates, glue or clear tape

In this activity, children use paper picture plates to work on beginning sounds.

First, help the child look through old magazines and find five or six pictures of objects, each of which is a different color (a red car, a green field, a blue pen, a black building, an orange vegetable, and so on). Cut out the pictures, and glue or tape each one onto a paper plate. Stack the plates. Ask the child, "Can you find a picture of something green?" Have the child find the green picture, identify the object, and say a word that has the same beginning sound. Continue through the entire stack of plates.

WORD PLAY

LETTER HOPSCOTCH

What You'll Need: Chalk, bean bag

Here's a letter game that's good for active children.

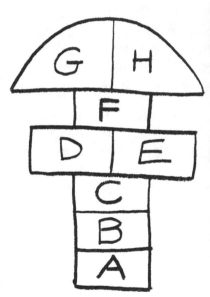

On a sidewalk or safe driveway, mark off a hopscotch game. Put a capital letter in each box as illustrated in the drawing. The child tosses the bean bag into letter square *A*, then hops over letter *A*, landing on each of the other hopscotch grid letters in succession. The child then turns around and hops into the letter squares in reverse order. From letter *B*, however, the child picks up the bean bag in letter square *A*, hops into that square, and then hops out of the grid.

On the next turn, the child throws the bean bag to letter *B* and hops from letter *A* to *C*, and so on, repeating the procedure as before. The child always hops over the box that has the bean bag in it, until picking up the bag on the return trip and hopping out of the grid.

PHONETIC FOOTBALL

What You'll Need: Construction paper, blunt scissors, marker or pen

Encourage sports lovers to practice beginning sounds.

Cut six football shapes out of construction paper. Print a different letter on each football. Place the footballs in a row. Have the child start at the left end of the row and say a word that begins with the sound of the letter on the football. Explain to the child that, to score a touchdown, he or she must reach the other end of the row by saying a word for each football's letter. Play again by adding new letters.

ALPHABET RHYTHM

Play a rhythm game that gives children practice in quick thinking and beginning sounds.

Illustrate a rhythm pattern involving clapping hands and stomping feet—for example: clap, clap, stomp, stomp. Have the child clap and stomp the rhythm with you. Then tell the child that, after going through the rhythm twice, you will say a word beginning with the letter *A* sound. Then you will repeat the rhythm twice again, and he or she will say a word beginning with the *B* sound. Continue taking turns throughout the alphabet.

With advanced players, start over when a player does not think of a word in rhythm. For beginners, keep repeating the rhythm until the player thinks of a word.

BUTTON, BUTTON!

What You'll Need: Construction paper or poster board, blunt scissors, marker or pen

Play this hiding game with a small group to give children practice with beginning sounds.

First, cut a "button" with a diameter of approximately 2 inches out of construction paper or poster board. On one side of the button, write a letter. Have players sit in a circle on the floor, and choose one player to be "it." The player covers his or her eyes while the other players pass the button around. After a minute or so, the player who is "it" says, "Button, button, who's got the button?" At this point, the player holding the button must hide it in his or her lap.

The player who is "it" then opens his or her eyes and tries to guess who has the button. If the guess is correct, the child who is "it" must identify the letter of the button and say a word in which that letter is the beginning sound. If he or she is correct, then the person hiding the button becomes "it."

NAME THAT CARD

What You'll Need: Deck of playing cards

In this game, children can learn the basics of playing card games as they work on beginning sounds.

Shuffle the cards. Show the child one card at a time, and say its number or name (jack, queen, king, ace). Have the child say a word that has the same beginning sound. If the answer is correct, give the child the card. Continue until the child has won several cards. As the child learns the names of the cards, he or she can say the name of each card, as well as a word with the same beginning sound.

BEAN BAG TOSS

What You'll Need: Old shower curtain or plastic tablecloth, marker, bean bag

This is a good activity for an energetic child.

Find a clean, old shower curtain or tablecloth. On an unprinted side, write the letters of the alphabet in scrambled order. Make the letters fairly large, but try to spread them out so that they are at least a few inches apart and cover most of the surface. Place this alphabet sheet on the floor. Give the child a bean bag, and ask him or her to toss it onto the sheet from several feet away. Have the child say the name of the letter closest to the spot where the bean bag lands.

Variation: Call out a letter first, and then tell the child to try to throw the bean bag so that it lands on that letter. Or, instead of saying a letter, say a word, then have the child identify the beginning letter and try to toss the bag on that letter.

CAREERS FROM A TO Z

What You'll Need: Large sheet of paper or poster board, marker or pen

Here's a project that relates to the question, "What do you want to be when you grow up?"

Help the child make a poster illustrating various careers. Begin with the letter *A,* and ask the child to think of a career whose name begins with that letter, such as *astronaut.* Have the child write the letter and draw a picture of an astronaut. Continue through the alphabet, skipping letters that don't work or do not bring an easy response.

CAT AND MOUSE

What You'll Need: Letter cards

Here's a game that will challenge a child to move quickly and quietly.

Have the child imagine that he or she is a mouse and that you are a cat. The "mouse" must take the "cheese"—a letter card—without getting caught by the "cat."

Sit in a chair. Place a letter card on the floor behind you. Close your eyes, and wait for the child to take the card. If you hear him or her, say, "I hear a mouse." If you speak before the child has picked up the card, he or she must take your place on the chair, and you must try to take the card. If the child takes the card without getting caught, he or she must name a word that begins with the letter on the card. The child then keeps the card, a new card is laid down, and the game is repeated. The player who successfully takes the most cards wins.

SPIN AND WIN

What You'll Need: Poster board, marker or pen, blunt scissors, paper fastener, six pictures of common items cut from an old magazine, index cards, glue or clear tape

This spinning game requires both luck and knowledge of beginning sounds.

On the poster board, draw a large circle and divide it into six sections. Write a letter on the edge of each section. Cut out a long spinner, and attach it to the center of the circle with a paper fastener. Next, make a set of six picture cards (pictures cut from old magazines glued or taped to index cards). Each card should show an object whose name begins with one of the letters on the circle. Shuffle the cards, and put them in a stack.

To play the game, a player spins the spinner and takes the top picture card from the pile. If the name of the picture begins with the letter sound he or she has spun, the player keeps the picture. If not, the next player spins. Continue taking turns until all the picture cards have been won.

PHONICS FUN FACT
The most common words in written English are *the, of, to, in, and, a, for, was, is,* and *that.* The most common words in spoken English are *the, and, I, to, of, a, you, that, in,* and *it.*

LETTER PALMS

What You'll Need: Newspapers, tape, blunt scissors, letter cards, paper clips

Surprise children with a "palm tree" made out of newspapers.

Roll a sheet of newspaper to the center of the sheet. Then add a second sheet so that its edge is at the center of the first sheet. Continue rolling the two sheets together, and put a piece of tape around the base to keep the tube from unraveling. Next, cut halfway down the tube you have made. Make three or four more similar cuts. Carefully pull up on the paper, and a "palm tree" will form.

Ask the child to randomly select a letter card from a stack of such cards. If the child can name a word with that beginning letter, he or she can clip the card to one of the paper palm fronds. Continue until the child has clipped several cards.

CONSONANT CANS

What You'll Need: Large coffee cans, plastic lids, marker

Children will learn beginning sounds with this grab bag activity.

First, make sure the coffee cans have no sharp edges. Print a consonant letter on the top of the can lid. Have the child look for objects whose names begin with that letter. For example, for the letter *P*, the child might find a peanut, postcard, pen, paper clip, and penny. Put the lid on the can, shake it up, and take turns removing and naming the items. Create cans with other letters.

FEED THE BIRDS

What You'll Need: Pinecones, two plastic dishes, peanut butter, bird seed, plastic spoon, yarn, bird book (optional)

Find some pinecones, and as you are collecting them with the child, talk about the types of trees that have pinecones and needles. See what different sizes and types of pinecones you can find.

When you return home, tell the child that you will make a bird feeder from the pinecones. Ask, "Do you know what birds like to eat that begins like the word *sun?*" (Answer: seeds.) Put some peanut butter in one dish and bird seed in another. Have the child take a plastic spoon and spread peanut butter on a pinecone. Then have the child roll the peanut butter-covered pinecone in bird seed. The peanut butter will make the bird seed stick to the pinecone.

When several bird feeder pinecones are made, take pieces of yarn and help the child tie a knot around the top of each one. Then make a loop at the other end of the yarn, and hang the pinecones on a tree branch. As you are hanging the bird feeders, ask the child, "What two things did you use to make this that begin like the word *pat?*" (Answer: pinecone and peanut butter.) "What did you put on the peanut butter-covered pinecone that begins like *sun?*" (Answer: seeds.)

Watch the tree, and observe how many different birds come to eat these treats. Use a bird book to help identify them.

NURSERY VISIT

Building one's vocabulary is a necessary part of language development. Visits to businesses offer valuable opportunities for a child to learn new words.

Visiting a garden nursery, the child learns that the word *nursery* does not always mean a place where babies or very young children are cared for. Upon arriving at a nursery, show the child the different types of plants, flowers, trees, shrubs, and other items that are available there.

Have the child select and purchase a plant to take home. Make sure the plant is suitable for a child and is nonpoisonous. On your way home, discuss what the child saw at the nursery and how to take care of the new plant. Discuss what the plant needs in order to grow. This can be done by saying, "I'm thinking of something that a plant needs to grow that begins with the letter *W*. What is it?" (Water.) Or: "I'm thinking of something that a plant needs to grow beginning with the letter *S*. What is it?" (Sun.)

PHONICS FUN FACT
Vowels vibrate in your throat (instead of being formed by a part of your mouth). You can test this by saying the five vowels aloud with your hand against your throat.

FARMER IN THE DELL

Play a favorite singing game to help children practice beginning sounds.

Sing "Farmer in the Dell." Start with the traditional verse: "The farmer in the dell, the farmer in the dell, hi-ho the dairy-o, the farmer in the dell." For the second verse, begin by saying, "The farmer takes a cat." Have the child sing new verses, adding a new word beginning like the word *cat* each time. For example, the third verse might be "The cat takes a *cow*" and the fourth verse "The cow takes a *carrot*."

After the child has sung several verses, change to a new letter, such as *D* ("The farmer takes a *dog*"), and continue.

BLOCK PARTY

What You'll Need: Set of building blocks with letters, paper, marker or pen

Here's an activity that makes children's play with building blocks even more instructive.

Print a word on a sheet of paper. Have the child find the blocks with the letters that spell the word and arrange them in order. Words to start with are *cat, dog, boy, top, big, fan, run, jump, play, ball,* and *girl*. As the child progresses, you might spell words with a theme, such as animal words or family words. You might also have the child spell the words.

NUTS AND BOLTS

On your next trip to the hardware store, have the child accompany you and discover the letters and letter sounds of the materials found there.

As you and the child stroll down the aisles of the store, stop and say, "I see something beginning with the letter *P*. What could it be?" (Answer: paint.) See how many different beginning letters you can find and name. Some items to look for are bolts, file, hammer, ladder, mailbox, nuts, rope, sandpaper, and wallpaper.

On your way home, talk about the many items that you saw at the hardware store and the different beginning-letter sounds of those things.

LETTER DROP

What You'll Need: Handkerchief

Give children practice identifying beginning sounds as they play "Drop the Handkerchief."

Have a small group of children stand in a circle. The child who is "it" takes the handkerchief, walks around the outside of the circle, and drops the handkerchief behind one player. That player must name a word and then tell the letter that makes its beginning sound. If the player is correct, he or she then becomes the player to drop the handkerchief. To make the game more challenging, you may want to give a category for the words to be named, such as vegetables, plants, or animals.